D0538543

ENDANGERED!

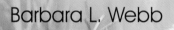

Barbara L. Webb

WITHDRAWN

ROURKE
PUBLISHING
www.rourkepublishing.com

www.rourkepublishing.com

PHOTO CREDITS: Cover ; Title Page © Ijaz Bhatti; Page 6 © Mableen; Page 7 © Jaime Pharr; Page 9 © VMJones; Page 11 © Paparico; Page 12 © Andrew F Kazmierski; Page 13 © Sondra Paulson; Page 14 © Catherine Kaufell; Page 15, 17 © U.S. Fish and Wildlife Service; Page 18 © Sina Georgy, KrivoTIFF, Yuliya Latysheva; Page 19 © Håkan Karlsson; Page 20 © Josef Muellek; Page 21 © Stephen Miller;

Edited by Meg Greve

Cover and Interior design by Tara Raymo

Library of Congress Cataloging-in-Publication Data

Webb, Barbara L.
 Endangered! / Barbara L. Webb.
    p. cm. -- (Green Earth Science Discovery Library)
 Includes bibliographical references and index.
 ISBN 978-1-61741-772-6 (hard cover) (alk. paper)
 ISBN 978-1-61741-974-4 (soft cover)
 Library of Congress Control Number: 2011924818

Rourke Publishing
Printed in the United States of America, North Mankato, Minnesota
060711
060711CL

www.rourkepublishing.com - rourke@rourkepublishing.com
Post Office Box 643328 Vero Beach, Florida 32964

Table of Contents

Endangered or Extinct?

Passenger pigeons used to fly over the United States in big groups. The very last passenger pigeon died in 1914. This **species** of bird is now **extinct**.

The last passenger pigeon, named Martha, lived at the Cincinnati Zoo until she died on September 1, 1914.

Today, about 25 blue iguanas survive in the wild. The blue iguana is **endangered**.

Humans are building homes and golf courses over the Venus flytrap's habitat. This plant may soon be endangered.

Endangered animals and plants might soon become extinct.

Nature, Humans, and Invaders

Plants and animals face danger from natural causes and human causes. Disease, disasters, and lack of food are natural causes.

The Tasmanian devil is endangered in part due to a disease it cannot resist.

Humans put plants and animals in danger by overhunting and **poaching**. Hunters have poached too many rhinoceros for their horns.

People in some countries want rhinoceros horns for decoration and medicine.

Humans also build houses and farms that destroy or change plant and animal **habitats**.

Humans have shrunk the habitat of the endangered giant panda.

Plants and animals then have a hard time finding enough food and space to survive.

Humans also release **invasive** plants or animals into habitats where they do not belong.

These invaders take food or space from other plants and animals.

Purple loosestrife is an invasive plant that grows quickly. It destroys the habitat of the endangered bog turtle.

The purple loosestrife can grow over wetland spaces the bog turtle needs for sunning and nesting.

Why Should We Help?

All plants and animals, including humans, depend on other plants and animals for survival.

Habitat
Restoration
Area

One endangered or extinct species can harm an entire **ecosystem**.

If ocean plankton became endangered, herring would not have enough to eat. Without herring in the ocean, the Orca whale would lose its food.

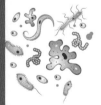

You Can Help...

- By asking governments to protect habitats.

- By keeping invasive plants and animals out of our gardens and homes.

- By volunteering with **conservation** groups.

The U.S. government made laws against using chemicals that made it hard for Peregrin Falcon eggs to hatch. This bird is no longer endangerd.

Try This

1. Help scientists count birds and animals to figure out how many are left. Learn how to participate in The Great Backyard Bird Count (http://www.birdsource.org/gbbc/kids).

2. Find out how you and your family can volunteer to remove invasive plants from your area. Your state's Department of Natural Resources (DNR) can help you get started.

3. Study the living things in your backyard. How are they connected? Can you create a picture that shows how one thing depends on another for survival? How are you dependent on these things? What would happen if one of these living things were to disappear?

Glossary

conservation (kahn-sur-VAY-shuhn): protecting natural habitats

ecosystem (EE-koh-siss-tuhm): an area in nature where plants and animals depend on each other for survival

endangered (en-DAYN-jurd): a plant or animal that is decreasing in numbers and is in danger of becoming extinct

extinct (ek-STINGKT): a plant or animal that no longer exists

habitats (HAB-uh-tats): the places where plants and animals live

invasive (in-VAY-siv): a plant or animal that has spread into a place it does not belong

poaching (POHCH-ing): to hunt or pick something in a way that breaks a law

species (SPEE-sheez): a group of plants or animals that are the same

Index

Websites

www.kidsplanet.org

www.dnr.wi.gov/org/caer/ce/eek/earth/endangered.htm

www.pbs.org/wnet/nature/episodes/the-loneliest-animals/introduction/4898/

www.nwf.org/kids.aspx

www.pandasinternational.org/kids.html

About the Author

Barbara L. Webb has lived in the Great Lakes region all her life and is very happy to hear that the endangered Lake Sturgeon is making a comeback. She is the author of five green science books for kids.